The Ordered Mind in A Disordered Society

The Art of Concentration and The Power of Concentrated Thought

Pedro De Silva

Contents

The Art of Concentration.

The art of concentration is one of the simplest to learn, and one of the greatest when mastered; and these pages are written especially for those who wish to learn how to master this fine art in all of its aspects; who wish to develop the power to concentrate at any time and for any purpose; who wish to make real concentration a permanent acquisition of the mind.

Whatever your work or your purpose may be, a good concentration is indispensable. It is necessary to apply, upon the object or subject at hand, the full power of thought and talent if you are to secure, with a certainty, the results you desire, or win the one thing you have in view. But the art of concentration is not only a leading factor in the fields of achievement and realization; it is also a leading factor in another field, a field of untold possibility.

The exceptional value of concentration is recognized universally; and still there are comparatively few that really know how to concentrate. Some of these have a natural aptitude for concentrated thought and action, while others have improved themselves remark- ably in this direction, due to increased knowledge on the subject; but as yet the psychology of concentration is not understood generally; and that is why the majority have not developed this great art, although they are deeply desirous of doing so.

When we do not know how to proceed, we either hesitate or proceed in a bungling fashion; or, we may proceed under the guidance of a number of misleading beliefs. And in connection with concentration there are several ideas and beliefs that have interfered greatly with the development of this art. In fact, methods have been given out, and published, that are supposed to develop concentration, but that produce the very opposite effect.

These things, however, clear up when we learn the psychology of the subject. Among these misleading beliefs, we find one of the most prevalent to be that we must, in order to concentrate well, become oblivious to everything but the one thing before attention now; but the fact is that when we become oblivious to our surroundings we do not concentrate at all; we have simply buried ourselves in abstraction, which is the reverse of concentration.

The mind is highly active and thoroughly alive when we concentrate perfectly; and sufficiently alive and keen to be aware of everything in the mind and all about the mind, although giving first thought and attention to the work in hand.

Another belief is this, that we must use great force in the mind in order to concentrate well; that is, we must literally compel the mind to fix attention upon the object or subject before it; but here we must note that forced action, although seemingly effective for a while, is detrimental in the long run. This is true of the body as well as of the mind, so that we must find a better method.

However, when we learn the real secret of concentration, we find that no special effort is required; there is neither mental strain nor hard work connected with the process; the mind becomes well poised and serene; and, in that attitude, full power and capacity is applied where attention is directed.

The mind that concentrates well does not work in the commonplace sense of that term; wear and tear have been eliminated; there is no strenuous action; there is no desire to force or drive things through; and no tendency whatever towards the high strung or keyed up condition. On the contrary, all action is smooth, orderly, easy and harmonious; and work has become a keen pleasure. This we can fully appreciate when we learn that, in real concentration, the mind has gained that peculiar faculty through which it can at will open all the avenues of energy in such a way that all those energies flow into one stream; and that stream flows into the one place where work is going on now.

Therefore, it is not a matter of main force, but a matter of knowledge; knowing how and where to open the gates of energy in the mental world. When we study the psychology of concentration, we find that most of our previous beliefs on the subject will have to be discarded. They have only acted as obstacles; and as those obstacles have prevented the development of real concentration, another obstacle has arisen in nearly every mind, that of adverse suggestion, the most detrimental of all.

Briefly, the majority, feeling the lack of concentration, continue to think and speak of this factor as weak.

They continue to suggest to themselves, ignorantly and unintentionally, that they are very poor in concentration; and therefore, they hold this factor down in a perpetual state of weakness. No mental faculty or power can develop to any extent so long as we think or speak of that faculty as weak or inferior. Adverse suggestion acts as a blight, and must not be permitted under any circumstance. We should think as little as possible about our weak points. When we know that we have a certain weakness, we need not speak of it further. To dwell mentally upon weakness is to live mentally in weakness; and they who live mentally in weakness cannot develop strength. Therefore, we will not think or say, again and again, that we are unable to concentrate, or that we are weak or inferior in any respect whatever. We will eliminate all manner of adverse suggestion. We will think and say that we can. We will not complain that we concentrate poorly, but we will proceed to train ourselves to concentrate wonderfully.

What Is Concentration?

Concentration in general may be defined as an active state of mind wherein the whole of attention, with all available energy and talent, is being applied upon the one thing that we are doing now. We concentrate in the full meaning of the term when we give ourselves completely to the thought or the action of the present moment; and this is true whether we work with muscle, brain or mind, or express ourselves through thoughts, words or emotion.

The principle of concentration is to do one thing at a time, and to do that one thing with all the talent and power we possess. We literally turn on the full current of mental and personal energy not only the full current of what we may feel on the surface of thought, but all that we can arouse in deeper consciousness, and bring forth from the greater self within. It is a leading purpose in concentration to lay hold upon deeper and greater possibility; for we are not giving our whole best self to the work in hand unless we apply all the life, energy and talent that we can through super-effort awaken and develop now.

How this may be accomplished we will understand clearly as we proceed with our analysis of the many phases of the subject; and we will discover that the power to concentrate well means vastly more and involves vastly more than most minds ever imagined. Although the general purpose of this art is to give undivided attention to the work in hand, the development of that purpose will presently lead us beyond this point, and we will enter a new field; we will discover in concentration a new power and a marvelous possibility.

There are many things that we may expect to accomplish through concentration; and in order that we may become familiar with this art from every aspect which is necessary to its highest development, we will consider briefly the most important of these accomplishments. First of all, we gain the power to hold attention upon any object or subject for a sufficient length of time to complete the work in hand, and the power to do this at any time and under any circumstances. This is vitally important as we all meet distractions at every turn, and must learn to give our work undivided attention whatever our surroundings may be.

When we concentrate well, we may, at will, cause all the available energies of mind and personality to work together, with full capacity, upon the work in hand. This will increase remarkably the working capacity and the dependable endurance of both mind and body, and will mean a high degree of mental mastery.

To be able to master the elements and energies of the mind sufficiently to bring them all together to work together anywhere any time this is an advantage for which we would pay almost any price; but it comes as a natural emolument with the development of concentration.

We all appreciate the value of speed, and especially among the thinking processes of the mind. The mind that moves slowly is never brilliant; while the mind that can think and act with lightning rapidity is on the verge of attaining genius; and may reach the goal of genius in this way if depth and range are combined with the element of speed. It is not possible, however, to produce mental speed through forced action; it comes naturally through concentration; and it will mean more work and better work; more perfect plans and more brilliant ideas, a combination that will go very far towards the high goal we have in view.

You are equal to any occasion when the whole of your mind is called into action; and this very thing concentration has the power to do. More than that, the whole of the mind will be called to higher ground, thereby working itself out of mediocrity and restricted channels, and gradually developing itself into that wonder state where everything seems possible. Real concentration can lead the way; the whole mind will follow; and concentration invariably leads into worlds of greater results.

When we concentrate well, we exercise a peculiar influence over the whole mind; we create, in every part of the mind, an irresistible desire to go to work; and we inspire every element of the mind with a definite ambition to excel.

The act of concentration tends not only to apply effectively all available energy of mind and personality; but tends also to draw forth latent energies. The fact is that real concentration becomes in the mind a remarkable force of attraction, attracting to itself unused and latent energies from all sources in the mental world. That is one reason why the mind that concentrates well becomes so powerful, and why such a mind will invariably forge ahead, regardless of what the obstacles or difficulties may be.

It is now a known fact that the subconscious supply of latent energy is enormous; and as concentration tends to attract latent energy from all sources, we perceive here possibilities that assume tremendous proportions. Concentrated action will grow into greater action, and upon the principle that "much gathers more"; "nothing succeeds like success"; "make expert use of what you have and Nature will bountifully increase your supply." All things in life flow into the main stream, because the main stream is going somewhere, concentrating its movements upon a definite goal.

Concentrate the mind upon any problem, and if you concentrate wonderfully well, you will find the solution. The solution of any problem is locked up in that problem; and concentration is the key. The psychology of this involves a most fascinating study; but sufficient in this stage of our study to know that these things can be done. The same is true of any subject, situation or circumstance.

9

You can, through concentration, find the main points or the inside facts of any subject or situation that you may consider. Real concentration has the power to break through the shell; to get beneath the surface; to get in behind the scenes; to enter into the very life of the thing, and thus get hold of bed-rock information.

These things we may accomplish through concentration; and there is good reason therefore why it has always been looked upon as the master art; but there is one thing more, the greatest of them all.

Mental action, when perfectly concentrated, tends to go farther and farther into the life, substance or principle that is acted upon at the time. Concentration develops a penetrating tendency a tendency to lead the mind out of the usual and on into the unknown. Concentration forges ahead. It goes straight on. It does not tarry with known facts. It goes farther. It sets out upon a journey; and such a journey will invariably prove a journey of discovery. The mind will find and enter new fields of thought. New laws and principles will be discovered. A new region of possibility will open before the mind, and long sought secrets may come to light.

Positively, we can, through a highly developed concentration, cause Nature to give up her secrets, and cause the mysteries of Life to be revealed.

The First and Most Vital Essential for Concentration.

When we realize what may be accomplished through concentration, we shall make every conceivable effort to develop this master art; and our persistence, determination and enthusiasm will know neither pause nor measure; we will purpose positively to learn how to concentrate, and therefore will want to know how to proceed, what principles to adopt, and what methods to apply.

When we examine the psychology of concentration, we find that it is based upon mental actions that are deeply interested in a certain subject or object; that is, we concentrate naturally and without effort whenever or wherever we are vitally interested. This then is the first principle. Be really interested in that to which you are to address yourself, and you will give it your undivided attention.

The problem, however, is how to become really interested in subjects or objects that do not, on their own account, attract our attention; or that do not, on the surface, appeal to us in the least. This is the first and possibly the greatest obstacle we have to meet in the development of concentration; but the solution is very simple; and we proceed upon the fact that everything is interesting from a certain point of view, that everything can attract our attention if permitted to reveal its chief attraction. To the superficial mind many things may seem useless or uninteresting; but not so to the mind that has learned to think. It is only on the surface, or from a commonplace viewpoint, that most things may seem unworthy of passing notice; and it is only when looked upon through the eyes of prejudice or ignorance that our associations may repel or produce indifference, or that life and its work may offer slight appeal. The situation changes entirely when we see

11

things as they are; and especially when we seek for the deeper cause of every condition and discover the greater possibilities that are awaiting back of the scenes everywhere.

The most commonplace object in existence, such as a simple rock or a turf, becomes a wonder-world when examined scientifically; and the ordinary duties of life, if examined from all points of view, will reveal opportunities and possibilities that will positively startle the mind. It is certainly true that everything is interesting from a certain point of view, and we may multiply illustrations in-definitely.

The universe in all of its realities; life in all of its manifestations; and existence in all of its actions and changes these things, when looked into, with eyes that see, will prove interesting to a wonderful degree, and frequently fascinating to an amazing degree.

Understanding this aspect of the subject, which is the all-important aspect, we may make the following proposition: We concentrate naturally and perfectly when we are vitally interested. Everything is, in its chief attraction, extremely interesting. Therefore, we may, by seeking the chief attraction in everything, concentrate naturally and perfectly anywhere at anytime. This is simple and conclusive, provided we find the chief attraction; but here we meet another problem. We may grant that everything is interesting from a certain point of view, but is it possible to find that interesting viewpoint anywhere and on short notice?

It is true that we can, in due time, find elements of real interest anywhere of sufficient interest to attract our undivided attention; but we may not al-ways do so at the moment; therefore, we have another problem to solve; and again, the solution is simple and within easy reach of anyone who will try. It is only necessary at first to proceed upon the conviction that everything is interesting from certain points of view; and to drill that fact into the mind with positive action and depth of thought. A situation will arise that can solve this other problem absolutely.

When you convince the mind that everything is interesting from a certain point of view, you establish, in the sub- conscious, a natural tendency to be on the alert for this interesting viewpoint. Your mind will, unconsciously and unfailingly, look for the interesting element in everything you meet in life, or that you may take up for consideration. And when the mind is on the alert, and keenly looking for the interesting element, the mind is really interested in that subject or object. Vital interest in the situation has sprung up subconsciously, without your making the least effort to become interested. So there you have the first and most vital essential for concentration.

The importance of this principle is so great, and the methods connected with it are so effective, that we should emphasize and reemphasize these things in our minds in every way conceivable. We should think on these things repeatedly; dwell upon this situation with the utmost of faith and confidence; and give special time and thought to the facts involved. There is a tendency in nearly every mind to take natural interest in a few things only; to work and act largely in grooves, and to think of things in the most general and superficial fashion. But real concentration is out of the question in such a state of mind; that is why special attention should be given to the facts under consideration, so that the tendency of indifference may be supplanted by one of whole-hearted interest.

In practical life this is how the plan will work. You are called upon to give attention to something you do not understand, or something that does not ap peal to you in the least. You are not interested, and therefore you cannot, at the moment, concentrate properly, or give the matter undivided attention. But you remember the great fact noted in this study, that everything is interesting from a certain point of view. Instantly you become curious to know what the interesting element in the matter in hand might be. You have made your own mind curious; and a curious mind is on the verge of becoming an interested mind.

If this be your first attempt in the application of this method, nothing more than a mild interest may arise; and even that might aid you decidedly at the time; but suppose you make use of this method many times every day for weeks and months. Suppose you make it a part of your daily work to impress upon your mind, again and again, the fact that everything is interesting from a certain point of view. The subconscious will soon receive these impressions and make that fact its very own. Then suppose you are called upon to consider a subject towards which you have been wholly indifferent. But the subconscious has been advised that there are elements of interest everywhere, and the subconscious never forgets what it has once really learned. Accordingly, the mind will be prompted, by powerful impulses from within, to seek the interesting elements in the subject before you; and, before you are hardly aware of the fact, this subject has become interesting and attractive. Suddenly, a keen desire has come over you to look into this subject thoroughly. You want to know. You are vitally interested. You are giving the matter undivided attention. You are concentrating perfectly in that direction.

When it becomes a part of your mind to know and feel that there are interesting elements in everything, and that everything, when looked upon with eyes that see, becomes a wonder-world, you develop a permanent faculty for looking into the vital elements in all things. You are interested, deeply and permanently, in the workings and possibilities of all aspects of life; you are wonderfully attracted to the real and the true everywhere; and therefore, you will instantly, and without effort, give your whole attention to anything that you may meet, or that you are called upon to consider. Wherever you think and act, you do so with your whole mind; you concentrate perfectly, not because you are trying to do so, but because you have developed that something in yourself that produces perfect concentration.

A Permanent Rule of Life.

To develop this idea further, and secure all possible results, we should make it one of the permanent rules of life to meet everything with the desire to discover its real worth and chief points of interest; and whether the element of interest be found or not, the act of looking for that element will create interest in the mind, thereby producing a certain degree of concentration. Whether we meet the commonplace or the exceptional, this rule should be rigidly observed; and whenever we have moments to spare, we should apply the rule definitely to any subject or object at hand, so that the mind may develop a permanent and a powerful tendency in that direction.

To illustrate, we may take an ordinary looking rock and ask ourselves what there is about this rock in which we may become interested. We would ask what this rock is composed of, how many elements it may contain, how they combine, how they are attracted to each other and how they happen to hold together. We might proceed asking questions, and we would find that we could ask anywhere from fifty to one hundred very interesting and most scientific questions about this very ordinary looking rock; and every one of those questions would arouse the deepest interest in the mind because they would be questions that would involve some of the greatest principles in science.

The same method may be applied in connection with any object or any subject we may wish to consider; and in every instance we shall be surprised to find how many points of interest will come forth to attract and even amaze the mind. The truth is, that if we are wide awake to the meaning and purpose of everything in existence, we shall not find anything to be commonplace or un-interesting. What appears to be uninteresting appears so simply because we have not taken the time to make an intelligent examination. The moment, however, that we really examine the thing itself, and look into its elements, its nature, its qualities, its powers, its possibilities and its very soul, we shall find so much that is interesting that we might occupy the mind for days, weeks and months in a deeper and further examination.

We shall find nothing to be of greater value as a daily practice than to take up objects or subjects, in which we are not actually interested, and direct the mind to look for interesting viewpoints, elements or factors in connection with those objects or subjects. We shall be richly rewarded, because we will not only find much that is interesting, but we will, through this practice, train the mind to look naturally for that which is of interest everywhere; and we know that there is nothing that adds so much to our fund of knowledge as the happy faculty of being able to look for facts, or for the truth everywhere; and the same faculty tends to develop, not only intellect, but all the finer mental faculties as well.

This practice will produce a permanent tendency in the mind to look for the interesting in connection with everything that we may see, or hear, or think about; and this tendency will expand and develop the mind, and place us in a position to secure direct or first-hand information from every experience and from every object or subject that we meet on the way. More than this, the same tendency will develop in the mind the faculty of searching for the chief essentials, or the real thing, that invariably exists in the actual life or soul of that with which we come in contact; and it is hardly possible to over-estimate the value of such a faculty, knowing as we do that the average mind skims over the surface continually, and seldom, if ever, discovers the real, vital principle involved anywhere. When we develop the faculty of finding the real thing, the real truth, the real principle, the real power, the real factors that exist in everything we meet in life, we have gained immensely.

Whenever we meet what does not seem interesting, we should proceed at once to examine that particular thing with a view of finding something of interest; and we will find it. And when we have work that does not seem interesting, work upon which we must concentrate in order to do it well, we should take up such work in the same attitude; that is, we should inquire deeply and scientifically as to what there is about such work that is in reality interesting.

This question coming up, will cause the mind to become interested; and at once concentration will begin. And as we continue this practice, the tendency to look for the interesting everywhere will become second nature; that is, concentration will have become a permanent power in the mind, and will act thoroughly and effectively of itself, wherever the mind may proceed to act. The rule is simple: Look for the interesting, and the mind becomes interested; and wherever the mind is interested, there you concentrate naturally and effectively; provided, of course, that you subconsciously feel that there are; interesting elements in everything; and, provided further, that your mind is keenly alive with the desire to know, to achieve, and to excel.

Controlling The Actions of The Mind.

A most important essential in the development of concentration is to learn to control the actions of the mind, all the leading actions, both objective and subjective; and although this may seem to be a difficult undertaking, it is really quite simple, for in fact we exercise this power almost hourly to some degree. We all have experienced moments when the forces of the mind seemed to be under perfect control, when it seemed as if we could move those forces, in any mode or manner desired, just as we move our hands or feet. And when we analyze our states of mind during such moments, we find that we are in deeper or closer touch with the finer forces of mind and personality, that is the secret.

To acquire the art of entering into this closer touch therefore must be our purpose; and to begin, it is deeper feeling that prepares the way for that desired state of mind.

Whenever we proceed to concentrate, we should try and deepen the feeling of all thought and all mental action; in fact, we should try and feel so deeply about everything that we think or do that the mind actually enters into the very spirit of the process; that is, into the undercurrents of mental life, those finer currents that determine results in everything that is being done. We may, when concentrating in a superficial manner, secure some slight results temporarily, but it is those deeper, finer, more penetrating currents that produce real results, and that alone have the capacity to produce extraordinary results.

Be sides, it is the consciousness of those finer currents that gives the mind the power to exercise complete control over all the actions and forces of the mental world, an attainment that is most important in the development of concentration.

You may find it a problem at times to enter into this state of deeper feeling; but you can, by giving special attention to the principle, master this situation absolutely; and the secret will be found in comparing the two ways of listening to music. When you listen to music and remain in a superficial state, you are simply aware of pleasing sound, but nothing more. However, if you are in a deeper state of mind at the time, wherein you can appreciate the very soul of music, you will not simply hear pleasing sound, but infinitely more.

Every tone of that music will actually thrill the atoms of your being, and arouse feelings in mind and soul that are so deep, so lofty and so beautiful that you could not possibly describe them. Briefly stated, your entire being would be alive with the deepest and finest and most sacred emotions, and the experience would be such that its effect would remain with you for weeks, months and possibly years.

This illustrates what happens when we meet experiences, or anything in life, in the attitude of deeper and finer states of mind. At such times we do not simply discern the surface of things, or come in mental contact merely with the outer meaning; we actually discern the very life of things, and come in mental contact with the very kingdom of the soul. We find that we invariably enter into this deeper feeling when we try to live every act, thought or experience that may appear in our world; and the reason why is found in the fact that whenever we try to live anything, we enter into the very life of that particular thing.

To develop the tendency to enter the deeper states of the mind, we should work in harmony with a leading law in the mental world; that is, the peculiar proneness of the mind to produce within itself any state, condition or tendency that we continue to desire with persistence and sincerity, it is the truth that your mind will do anything for you if you really want it done.

19

When we make it our purpose to enter into deeper states of feeling in connection with every thought and action, the mind will soon develop a tendency that will invariably take all mental action into deeper states of feeling.

To encourage the mind in this connection, we shall find it a most excellent practice, whenever we hear good music, to look for the soul of music, to try and feel the finer touch of the real life of music, and to try to appreciate the most delicate harmonies that exist in the very spirit of music itself.

We shall find it an excellent practice to apply the same principle in connection with anything that is beautiful, or anything that may appeal to the mind as being worthy of our deepest and highest attention; and in fact, whatever we may be thinking about, we should try and enter into the very soul of the thought or the theme.

In this manner, we will develop a natural desire to seek for the real, to enter into the depths of life, thought and feeling; and gradually consciousness will deepen all of its activities until we find we can feel more deeply in every thought or experience; and we shall also find that the conscious domain has been increased remarkably.

We shall find it profitable to apply the same principle to every aspect of physical sensation, and to every experience of the sense life. If we make it our aim, not to be satisfied with the grosser side of physical sensation, but try to discern and feel the finer elements that are invariably expressed through all forms of sensation, we shall not only find every sensation more delightful than before, but also that it has been lifted to a higher plane where grossness and crudeness have disappeared, and that the physical body, as a whole, has become more refined in every form and manner.

These exercises and experiences will tend directly to prepare the way for the development of those states of mind that we must possess in order to enter into this closer and finer touch with the higher and finer forces of the mind, a most important essential in the art of controlling all the actions of the mind; for we know that when we have gained perfect control over all the actions of the mind, then we shall be able to concentrate all the energy we possess upon any object or subject we may have in view.

The purpose must be to live beneath the surface; to make the great within our chief realm of life and concern. We may act upon and with the external aspects of life; but we must make the deeper fields of thought our real place of business. For surely if we would master the deeper forces of life, we must live and think where those forces arise and develop. This, therefore, is a matter of imperative importance.

A Good Strong Will.

An indispensable element is that of a good strong will; and the use of the will in connection with concentration may be illustrated variously; but we will first examine the effect of will power, correctly applied, in the process of thought creation. To illustrate, we will suppose that you have several facts concerning a proposed invention, but have not as yet succeeded in bringing those facts together in the combination required for the perfecting of that invention. If you understand the use of the will, you will apply will power upon that group of facts, knowing that you thereby increase mental activity in that particular part of the mind; and wherever mental activity is increased, there the creative process is intensified and expressed to a higher and more perfect degree.

The fact is this, that whenever an idea may seem indistinct, although you know you have all the elements required, the reason is that the mind is not sufficiently active in connection with the creative process that is working to perfect that idea. The use of the will, however, will not only increase activity throughout this creative process, but will also make concentration more perfect, because the power of will, when applied in connection with concentration, increases invariably both the power and the capacity of the force of concentration.

You will find it possible to perfect almost any idea you have in mind, if you can bring to bear upon that idea all the available energy existing in your mind; and this may be accomplished through concentration, provided concentration is deeply expressed, and in a positive manner. For when we fully apply the will, we increase power and activity. We intensify the process involved; and there is nothing that tends more directly to increase the power of concentration than the act of increasing the rapidity of action wherever concentration may be taking place.

We all appreciate the value of brilliant ideas; and most minds are in a position to create brilliant ideas at frequent intervals, but as a rule they merely come up to the point of creating a brilliant idea; they do not quite reach the point itself. The reason is that they have not the power to bring together all the elements required for this new idea; and this power is lacking because the will is weak and concentration undeveloped.

The same is true regarding the perfecting of plans or methods. We may have the essentials, or all the factors required, but we may not always have the power to bring them together to a focus, where the required combination can be brought about so as to evolve the idea or plan we desire. The use of the will, however, in this connection will produce remarkable results. The will always intensifies any mental process, and thereby tends to bring to a climax any creative process that may be going on in the mind. The creation of rich and valuable thought may be furthered in the same manner, because such thought is almost invariably the result of the bringing together, in the proper combination, of the best impressions that may have come into the mind through our own study or experience.

Regarding the psychological use of the power of thought, we shall find the same principle of exceptional value, because whenever we use the power of thought, whether for the overcoming of physical ailments, for the elimination of adverse mental states, or for the building up of character or mental faculties, wherever we may apply the power of thought, a perfect concentration is indispensable; and the use of the will in connection with concentration invariably tends to increase both the force and the capacity of the process. In fact, we never can concentrate with all that we are unless we express through concentration, the full power of the will. To express the full power of the will, however, every action of the will must be positive, and the will must act subjectively; that is, it must act through the undercurrents, or through the attitude of finer feeling. The importance of which we have previously considered. We understand therefore that if we would learn to concentrate well, we must also acquire a thorough knowledge of the will, and develop the will to the highest possible degree.

The Power of Persistent Desire.

The power of persistent desire is invaluable wherever increased results are wanted; and therefore, the full force of desire must invariably combine with concentration. When we desire persistently the object in view, we become deeply interested in that object and we cause the whole mind to work for its realization.

Besides, the element of desire will instill something into concentration that is really alive. It will eliminate the tendency to make mental or personal actions mechanical or forced, and will give to every action that vital spark that means so much. The force of desire will also deepen and expand every mental process involved, a situation that may, at times, become the opening way to remarkable results.

To concentrate successfully we must direct and focalize all the creative energies of the mind upon the object of concentration; but these energies must first be aroused; and here is where real desire becomes invaluable. Wherever we turn on the full current of persistent desire, every energy and force in the mind becomes alive, and may be enlisted for good work in any place where the power of concentration has been directed.

We find therefore that the force of desire becomes a direct and powerful aid to concentration in two distinct particulars; first, by creating wide-awake interest all through the mind by causing the mind to become vitally interested in the goal in view; and second, by arousing, or making alive, the latent or dormant energies of the mind, thereby providing the process of concentration with a vast amount of additional power.

All of this we understand perfectly; and the more we investigate the psychology of the process, the more reasons we find why we always get what we want when we want it "really bad." The secret then is to want what you want with all the life and power there is in you. We can reach any goal, or realize any ideal when we concentrate perfectly, and with the full force of a perfect concentration; and persistent desire proceeds to give concentration more and more of the two chief essentials; that is, deeper mental interest and greater mental power.

In this connection inquiry may arise as to the best methods for creating this deeper and more persistent desire, especially where we may not be personally interested in the final results; but here we should remember that we always gain personally from anything that is done right. If we develop greater oriental power through the use of any psychological law, we gain to that extent, even though the greater portion of the tangible results may, in this instance, go elsewhere.

The future is long; every form of gain will come to each one of us in due time, and in a very short time if we take advantage of every opportunity to increase our own capacity and power. We should therefore be interested, personally, in the best and most thorough use of every psychological law we may have the privilege to employ.

Realizing this fact, we will want to desire success, the greatest possible success for every enterprise with which we may be connected. Such a desire will improve remarkably, not only our own concentration, but also all other powers and talents we may possess. Our own gain therefore will be strictly personal, and most direct; and although tangible gain may not come at once, it positively will come in the near future. The future is both larger and richer for those who improve themselves in the present; and greater opportunities are waiting everywhere for greater minds; but improvements must be genuine, not merely superficial.

To increase the power of desire we should deepen and intensify all such desire in every form and manner, realizing the fact that the more the mind acts in a certain direction the greater becomes its power to act still more in the same direction. The force of desire therefore may through this simple rule become immense. And the more we increase the force of desire the more we increase results in every field of thought or action. Furthermore, we may cause the forces of concentration and desire to act and react upon each other to great advantage; that is, the more we concentrate for the increase of desire, worthwhile desire, the more powerful and persistent will such desire become; and the more deeply we desire the power to concentrate well, wonderfully well and the more life, energy and action we express in the building of real concentration.

The Faculty of Imagination.

The greatest faculty of all is that of imagination; but it is the least understood, due principally to the fact that most minds have remained in grooves of thought, and therefore have not given extensive attention to their own creative possibilities, the richest and most numerous of which exist in the fields of imagination. In the development of any power or talent, however, these creative possibilities must receive direct and scientific attention; and this is especially true with regard to the power of concentration. Besides, some of the functions of concentration are so closely related to those of imagination as to seem almost identical.

When you employ the faculty of imagination, one of your chief objects is to bring together ideas or mental images with a view of creating some new or greater idea; and in concentration this "bringing together" tendency, this uniting the many in one, is the leading object in view. It is clearly evident therefore that a better training of imagination will largely increase the power of concentration.

When you employ the faculty of imagination, you also tend to bring together the many creative energies of the mind, combining those energies in the one process to which you are giving attention at the time. A highly developed faculty of imagination therefore naturally becomes an invaluable aid to the power of concentration; and when we understand how concentration can, by working with imagination, bring together, into one powerful line of mental action, all the best ideas of the mind and all available creative energy, we know why we usually find an excellent imagination wherever we find a remarkable concentration.

Analyzing the subject farther, we find that a vivid, well-trained imagination tends to " light up " the entire mental world; or, in other words, to make everything in the mind clearer. The result is, that the idea or object upon which we concentrate becomes more distinct; and accordingly, we not only concentrate better, but the entire mind becomes interested in this idea on account of its vividness and distinctiveness.

Thus, we call into action the many aspects of mental attention, an action that increases directly and instantaneously the power of concentration. We all know through experience how much better we can think when the ideas with which we are dealing are vivid, or stand out clearly in the mind; and also, how much better we can concentrate when we have a distinct mental picture of the object in view. And imagination, if well trained and scientifically applied, will invariably turn the light upon any idea that we may call up for examination or further development.

When imagination is vivid, every mental process will be literally filled and surrounded with light; and we all can appreciate what an immense advantage this will be in the practical application of concentration. To illustrate, we will call imagination into action wherever we wish to concentrate, and immediately that place or process in the mind will become so vivid, and stand out so clearly, that all our faculties will become interested. The entire mind will turn its attention towards the point of concentration; and in a moment the en- tire mind will concentrate. And when we have the whole mind working for the object in view, the results desired will positively be realized.

As a practical suggestion we should, whenever we begin to concentrate, proceed to imagine all the forces of the mind coming to a focus at the point of concentration. This simple rule will not only produce some startling results in the process of concentration itself, but will also train imagination for definite and practical work. Herewith, let us note that imagination does have the power to take the lead in the mental world; and therefore, whenever we imagine that a certain thing is being done in the mind, we lead a majority of the energies of the mind to go and do that very thing; provided of course that imagination be vivid and highly positive in its actions. Here then we have within easy reach a most remarkable possibility.

To Awaken More of The Mind.

To concentrate well is not sufficient; we must also concentrate with the greatest possible capacity; and therefore, we should train ourselves to concentrate with the whole mind; or to express more and more of life and power in every thought and action. But the average mind makes actual use of only a small fraction of what is possible in ability and power; and that is one reason why the concentrated efforts of such a mind are so weak or utterly futile.

Where concentration is weak and imperfect, we always find most of the mind in a dormant state; and vice versa, where concentration is exceptional, we find marked activity all through the mental world. The problem then is to awaken more of the mind, and express more of the power of the mind in everything we do, a problem that would largely solve itself if we would abandon completely all half-hearted modes of thought and action.

We should make it a practice to express the whole self in everything we do, think or say; and the increase in mental capacity would be remarkable. We should eliminate indifference absolutely. Whether we turn to the left or to the right, we should turn with all we have in feeling, purpose and will. Wherever we act, we should be a power, and aim to make all action constructive, conducive to greater capacity for action tomorrow. There is no gain in saving up power for another day. If we use it all now, we will have still more when the other day arrives. The power that is generated in the system today should be used today, not scattered but used, used in constructive expression. And the law is, that the more power we use today, the more power we will have tomorrow.

When we think, we should not simply think with the brain, but think with every force and element in the entire personality. There is nothing that will increase mental capacity so quickly and so effectively as the training of the mind to use the whole personality in every thought and expression. And when the mind can, in concentration, draw upon the entire personality for power, conscious and subconscious, we can imagine what the force of such concentration will be.

Our principal object, therefore, should be in this connection to awaken the vast regions of dormant energy all through the mental world, and express more and more of this new energy in everything we do. Thus, we provide concentration with an ever-increasing measure of power.

A most excellent practice, in order to express more of the mind in every thought and action, is to lay hold upon all the energy of the mind with deep feeling and will, and actually take up that energy as we would take up a book with the hand, and place it where we want it now. This can readily be done; and with practice we will find that we can control our mental energies just as effectively as we control the movements of hands or feet. When this control is gained, we shall be able, at any time, to increase the expression of the power of mind, thereby increasing directly the power of concentration; and when we realize that even exceptional minds use less than five per cent of their latent energies, we gain some idea of the vastness of our own possibilities.

To further this increase in mental capacity, we should give definite and frequent directions to the subconscious for this particular purpose. In fact, there is nothing that will avail so much for such a purpose, which fact we can readily appreciate when we note what the subconscious is, and what it can do. We should make it a daily practice there- fore to direct the subconscious to awaken the whole mind, and to express, in constructive action, the full power and capacity of the mind. Remarkable increase will be realized, as the weeks pass, both in working capacity and in thinking power.

Then we should proceed farther and direct the subconscious to develop and perfect concentration itself; and we shall be amazed at what can be done in this regard. We know that the subconscious can do anything within the range of human possibility, if properly directed; therefore, the creative power of the great within can build for us all the most effective and the most perfect concentration conceivable. This marvelous power is latent in every mind waiting to be used with intelligence, super-effort and real faith.

The Forces of The Mental World

In the science and art of concentration, it is the deeper forces and the finer energies of mind and personality with which we deal directly; and therefore, we increase the power of concentration as we acquire the ability to take up or control those forces at will, and according to our purpose or desire. To accomplish this, we must gain interior hold of those forces, because they do not respond to any action of mind or will that be merely superficial. And here we find another reason why it is only the few who really can concentrate; it is only the few who think deeply and who cause the actions of the mind to work among the powerful undercurrents of life, thought and mentality; but anyone can acquire this power; and the first step towards that end is to gain this interior hold of the finer energies of the mind.

When we can take hold of the forces of the mental world, and direct or sway those forces in any way desired, just as we sway or extend the arm in any mode or direction desired, when we can do this, then we are beginning to acquire the power of real concentration. This inner mastery of the forces and energies of the mind, is a purely subjective process, and is developed only as we learn to act consciously and positively in what we may term as "the inner field of thought" thought, consciousness and mind action. And although there are many who can and do act, to some extent, in this inner field, the majority can acquire this power only through extensive practice.

The value of this power, even aside from that of concentration, is very great, especially in connection with the creation of effective and brilliant ideas; for the fact is, that it is only in this inner field of mind and thought that brilliant ideas are created; and besides, every mental creative process of genuine worth depends directly upon the action of these finer energies. If we would develop the real power of concentration, therefore, and also master the art of creating brilliant ideas, we must think and act in the consciousness of the " inner field " of mentality, and gain, more and more, this interior hold upon the forces of mind and personality.

To advance in this direction, we should endeavor frequently to take up and apply the deeper forces of the mental system; that is, to take positive hold of those forces with mind and will, directing them first upon one sphere in the mental world, then upon some other sphere; to move those forces to and fro as we may desire; to cause them to move in circles one moment and in straight lines, either towards the depths or the heights of the mental world, the next moment; to gather them in large groups or in small groups according to desire; to focalize them all upon any subject or idea we have in mind, and to see how long we can continue such focalization without losing interest in the subject or becoming oblivious to our surroundings. And here we should remember that the moment we lose interest in the subject before us, that moment we cease to concentrate; and also, that the moment we become oblivious to our surroundings, that moment we cease to concentrate.

Concentration involves, on the one hand, undivided attention to the subject or object before us; and, on the other hand, complete wide-awakeness to everything going on among our surroundings. The moment we become oblivious to our surroundings, the real power of concentration is lost for the time being; it is very important therefore that we continue to be wide-awake, both to the objective and to the subjective; in fact, in as wide and deep and large a sphere as possible.

To gain this interior hold upon the deeper forces of the mind, it is continuous practice that will give the power desired; and every imaginable method should be employed, because the more ways through which we can handle, sway or manipulate those forces, the greater will become our conscious hold upon those forces; and when this conscious hold becomes remarkable, then we can apply those forces anywhere at any time, and with full capacity and power. In other words, we shall be able to concentrate perfectly, and turn on the full current of all the talent, energy and power we possess.

An excellent practice is to turn attention frequently upon the great within, concentrating the deeper forces of the mind upon the vast and marvelous possibilities that exist in the fathomless depths of the mental world. This practice will not only aid the mind remarkably in gaining this interior hold upon the finer energies, but will also awaken latent forces and new talents; and will invariably arouse increased capacity and power in every faculty and talent we may be using now.

When we find that the faculties and talents, we employ do not possess sufficient force and capacity to make that work a success, it is most important that we take up the above practice and do so with determination and enthusiasm. We will soon experience most marked improvement; the mental engine will have more " steam," and we shall be able to speed on with twice and thrice the usual cargo of plans, propositions and achievements. Furthermore, this practice will enlarge immensely the field for concentration; and here it is important to remember that the greater the scope and range of the mental world, of which we are actively conscious, the greater becomes the power of concentration.

Every faculty or power in the mind gains exceptional advantages when given more and more to work with; and the practice of concentrating frequently upon the great within will give every faculty more to work with, besides giving the mind, as a whole, an ever-increasing world for attainment and achievement.

The Possibilities of Concentration.

The possibilities of concentration are many; but there is one possibility in particular that we all should seek to understand most thoroughly, and develop to the highest degree conceivable. The results will be amazing; and every step in advance will open new worlds to conquer.

The principle is this, that we can through concentration clear the way for almost any achievement, attainment or discovery within the range of human life and power; and this range is a thousand times greater than we have supposed; in fact, no limits or restrictions can be found.

This principle can be applied to al- most anything that we may wish to find or accomplish; and for practical illustration we will consider first the problems we meet in daily life. It is the usual custom, when we have difficult problems to solve, to waste a vast amount of time and energy worrying about how we are to find the solution; and as we know this is an easy way to failure and defeat.

The new way is to concentrate; to concentrate upon the problem with all the energy and intellect we possess; and this is what will happen: The full light of the mind will be focused upon that problem; that problem will be placed under the penetrating gaze of a powerful mental search light; and, accordingly, the mind will be able to look into and look through the entire situation. Thus, the solution will be found; for the fact is, that situations or problems seem difficult or perplexing only when viewed in the dark or in subdued light. When we can look through the thing, then we know what to do.

Turn on sufficient light and all mystery disappears. Problems cease to be problems when viewed in the clear light; and we can, through a highly developed concentration, turn the full light of the mind upon any subject, circumstance or situation. Therefore, we should concentrate upon those things; concentrate with all the energy and intellect we possess; concentrate for days or weeks, if necessary, and with unflinching faith and determination. We will soon penetrate the mystery and find what is wanted. We will see through it all, and see clearly what to do.

The same principle will apply if you are working on some invention. Do not give up at any stage; concentrate upon the thing you wish to develop or perfect; and concentrate with more and more persistence until the thing is done. Nothing is impossible. Nature will give up her secrets to those who really want them, or to those who will come into her greater realms and get them; and concentration has the penetrating power to go on in anywhere.

It is a well-known fact that most inventions have come through persistent concentration; or through mental processes that involved lightning speed creative power; and such processes are always due to previous moments of exceptional concentration. Furthermore, the possibilities of the mind become simply marvelous when the full light and the full creative power of the mind are concentrated upon the goal in view. We realize therefore that greater inventions than the world has ever dreamed of may be expected when a much larger number learn to master the wonder working art of concentration.

Inventive genius involves, among other things, the power to create new ideas; and we can realize that the more intellect and energy we apply in any creative process the greater and more brilliant will that idea become. We also realize that when we apply all our faculties and forces upon the creation of an idea or the perfecting of an invention, the results will be far greater than if we applied only a fraction of those faculties and forces. And it is the function of concentration to apply, upon the work in hand, the full power of the mind and the highest and most effective actions of that power.

Rich things grow where producing power is abundant; and the producing power of the mind at any point will be abundant in profusion when we concentrate the best that we have and the best that we are upon that point. And to emphasize this fact, let us note again that the power of concentration when persistent and highly developed, will not only cause all the talents and forces of the mind to work together at the point of action, but will also awaken latent energies in mind and personality, sometimes an enormous amount of new energy, until you feel as if you were a living dynamo.

When you are in need of a new plan in your business, or in your field of endeavor, do not consult all the people you know, the majority of whom may not be really interested. That is the old way, and it leads to confusion. The new way is to concentrate upon the plan you want, and with the highest and greatest actions of the mind. Thus, you cause the highest and greatest in your mind to go to work and evolve the plan you desire. They can do it; and if you concentrate exceptionally well, you will cause those actions to make a super-effort the result of which will go far beyond your every expectation. Here you should note well the fact that your own mind has the power, active or latent, to work out any plan you may require for your best welfare and continued progress.

Nothing is truer than this, that your own mind is fully able to take the very best care of you. This is a statement that should be shouted from the house tops, and drilled so thoroughly into every human brain that it becomes a positive and ever conscious realization. Your own mind can solve your problems and work out the plans that you need for advancement in your life and your work. And your own mind will do these things if you concentrate persistently upon that which you want, and concentrate wonderfully well.

A large and valued field for the application of the same principle, is the field of ideals. And in this connection, we should consider well the great fact that whenever the mind gains the insight to perceive an ideal it also gains the power to make that ideal real. But it is only through a well-developed concentration that this power can be applied effectively. The majority, however, among those who entertain high ideals, do not give sufficient thought to concentration. They dream and dream, hoping the dream will come true; or, when they do try to concentrate, they journey off into abstractions and transcendental speculations, a process that does not call into action the power that is able to make those dreams come true.

The same is true of young minds who are ambitious. Most of them merely hope and hope that their ambitions will be realized somehow; but they do not concentrate persistently and continually upon the great goal they have in view. They do not call into concerted and organized action the sum total of their forces and faculties; and, in consequence, their ambitions never materialize.

The fact is that where one ambitious mind scales the heights of achievement, fifty give up their early ambitions after a few years and decide to resume an average existence; and the chief reason is, that these fifty do not concentrate; or, if they do concentrate, it is only for a time and in a weak, un-certain fashion. The successful one, however, turns on the full current of concentration, and persists, with un-daunted faith and determination, until the goal in view is realized.

This should be the rule: Whatever you want, concentrate; concentrate upon the purpose you have in mind; concentrate upon those greater forces and possibilities within you that can get you what you want, that can see you through successfully. For it is positively true that your own mind can get you anything within reason; provided of course that your whole mind is working for you; and your whole mind will work for you, will work for you with the highest degree of effectiveness if you concentrate wonderfully well.

The possibilities of concentration are not confined, however, to the usual fields of achievement, or to those mental domains with which most of us are familiar. There are other and greater worlds that we may discover and take possession of through the use of this master art. To illustrate, if we wish to evolve or develop something that is entirely new, or decidedly different, the principle is to concentrate in that direction. Thus, we shall make a super-effort in that direction; that is, if we concentrate with full capacity and marvelous skill; and we will, with absolute certainty, develop something that is beyond all previous effort, something that is distinctive, that stands out in a class by itself, that reveals clearly the master touch of genius.

The elements of genius are latent in every mind; and any mind may, through the super-efforts of a marvelous concentration, call those elements together into positive, creative action. Thus, something new or startling may be developed. It may be a new and most brilliant idea; or, a new and superior plan for the realization of certain highly desired changes in life; or, an entirely new way of doing things, ways and methods, which when applied, might revolutionize everything in that sphere of human thought or endeavor.

The most wonderful possibility of all is this, that concentration can lead the mind on and on, out of present restrictions and beyond present states of knowledge and consciousness, into new realms, richer kingdoms and greater worlds. We know that concentration does have the tendency to go farther; and that it has real penetrating power, so that it may delve into anything in the vast domains of Life, Mind or Nature. It is possible therefore to cause the power of concentration to go so far into any state of reality that new and marvelous domains will open before the mind. Thus, we might find long sought secrets in the natural world, or make discoveries in any field or region that would prove amazing to the mind and invaluable to human progress.

It is the positive truth that a highly developed concentration can carry the mind farther and deeper in any direction. This is something that the great minds of every age have demonstrated repeatedly. And if we go deeper or farther into Life, into Mind, into Nature, we are going to make discoveries.

We are going to find secrets that no mind has known before. We are going to meet forces, laws and principles, the knowledge of which may reduce to simplicity a thousand so-called impossibilities. We are going to discern the inner workings of things in many fields and regions, and thus secure information that wise men have sought all through the ages.

These things are not exaggerations nor the mere picturing of a highly stimulated imagination; for when we accept the fact that concentration can lead the mind farther and deeper in any direction, which fact we all accept absolutely, we realize that we may, through this use of concentration, discover or accomplish almost anything; that is, if we carry on the process far enough. It is a matter therefore of deciding to concentrate until we find or secure what we want. The outcome will be as expected; for in due time we shall meet the great and the wonderful; we shall learn how this remarkable power can open to the mind regions beyond regions of untold possibility.

Here then is food for thought whatever our work may be, or whatever our fields of study may be. Here we have promises rich and rare for those who aspire to excel; for those who are looking for new worlds to conquer; for those who are in search of the deeper secrets of life everywhere. And as we give thoughtful attention to these things, we perceive most keenly that we are ever on the brink of wonders and marvels, with the power to go on into those fabulous regions and take possession.

To the practical mind it is clearly evident that if we train the mind thoroughly along all essential lines, and learn to concentrate wonderfully well, we are going to move forward steadily and surely, gaining capacity, power and speed as we proceed. And if we continue in this manner, we will not only accomplish what we have in view, but we may at any time strike a new trail leading directly and quickly to the highest pinnacle of achievement.

To the mind of ideals, and to all who have faith in greater possibilities, it is equally evident that a well-trained mind can, through a highly developed concentration, take a charmed journey into Nature's wonder world, with the positive assurance that something of untold value will be found. For when we realize that the mind holds marvels and possibilities far beyond what we ever dreamed; and when we know that these mental marvels can be gathered and trained for super-effort, for creative work on any scale, or for going out upon expeditions of discovery, even entering into the secrets of life and the heart of things, when we note these things, we stand amazed at what might be done. But the mind of faith and courage will stand amazed only for a moment.

Such a mind will resolve to master this wonder art at once, for in it there is a power that never knew failure nor defeat, a power that is fully able to cast the mountains of impossibility into the sea of oblivion.

www.ingramcontent.com/pod-product-compliance
Lightning Source LLC
Chambersburg PA
CBHW070131290526
45789CB00005B/2206